Born Again Christian

Series 1

A Collection of Poetry

By

Tonya Latrice Wilson
Berwyn IL, usa

Born Again Christian-Series 1

© 2009 by Tonya Latrice Wilson

ISBN: 9780982931745

Printed in the United States of America

Dedication

This book is dedicated to GOD, the one that I can trust and believe in.

Table of Contents
Poetry by Tonya Latrice Wilson

John 3:7

"Do not marvel that I said to you, you must be born again."

Preface

This poetry was created and was born in order to Inspire, and to celebrate the re birth of salvation, and my new Life in Gods Kingdom.

Church Folks

Church Folks

That sister wearing her

pretty dress in church

should not be ignored:

That sister wearing

her pretty dress and her

fancy heels should be

adored. She is truly

called, somebody say

amen!

The entire church

should stand up from

their seat, and go and

shake that sister's hand!

With expensive clothes

like hers she got to be

saved, you see, she just

got to be free.

She can not be bound,

and has got to be living

pretty good: She

got to be living; just like

a God Fearing woman

should. Some say her

hat alone cost her 1500

dollars: They say that

she got about 1500

Followers:

That sister that is

wearing that $1500

dollar hat must Not be

poor, and must be

walking in the light:

That sister wearing hat

pretty dress, fancy high

heel shoes, and wearing

that 1500 Dollar hat

must be living right!

I Will Pray for you

I will pray for you

I had a choice to give up on you

I knew that you might be
going away soon.

With your life, the game
was already over before it even
began.

I was getting tired of hearing
bad news and never seeing you
progress.

I have an empty room in my heart,

where I have been praying for
you from the start.

My empty room is a like a

dynasty of love for you, boo,

and on this earth, and in the

past, I kept it real with you, I

told you the truth

Now I cannot save you,

because you still got that slave in

you.

You think that it is cool to

live a sad, depressing life.

You think it is cool to go to prison

and be apart from me, but not the

strife:

I want to hate you but the God in me

won't let me, and the Angel that walks

above my head won't even address the

word hate.

I have a choice to give up on you,

and to walk away. On the other hand,

I could just

Forgive you for your past mistakes.

However, after talking with you one

last time, I have decided to listen to the

voice of God, that lives inside of my heart

and to do just like the angels in Heaven

do.

I have decided that I will not stop

praying for you.

Stairway to Paradise

.

Stairway to Paradise

One black day, I was so tired of

Sitting alone in the crowd,

With my head down, feeling

Overwhelmed, as if, I may just

drown, in my own earthly cloud of

Grieving gloom:

On this particular day, I

realized that this world is filled with

sad and sorrowful people-that often

shine the bright light, on doom.

In addition, I know that we

live in a world where many

people do not Know God, and

do not know where to start,

because they are still Living

and feeling in the part of

their heart that is dark.

However, I do believe there is

a better place that we will face:

Better then Material things and

expensive rings: I do believe there

is, a better world.

Therefore, I am joyful and

boastful that I read about a

place that will have only day,

only light, and that will no

longer have night.

In addition, a place that will

have a new Heaven, And a new

Earth and I am not talking about any

church.

One black day, I was so tired

of sitting alone, in the crowd,

with my head down, feeling

Overwhelmed, as if,

I may just drown, in my own
earthly cloud of grieving gloom.

One black day, when I could
not sleep, and would barely
eat, because I was weeping
and grieving for my Pastor,
whom was as a Leader of his
sheep,
Yet, I was trying not to weep.
I believe that was the day that
the sky no longer, just looked blue,
but it looked brand new,

Moreover, I felt like I had

finally received the truth.

In addition, that was the day

that my mind received a new

kind of a light: and was no

longer in the dark, and I said

goodbye to the fog, so that I

could make some more room

in my heart.

Finally, I put away the

weeping eyes, the lies and the

tears, and Asked for the Lords

forgiveness. Moreover,

repented for my sins:

I felt like –that day, that my
eyes saw beyond the stars: I read
about a New Heaven and a New
Earth: I read about Paradise: I read
about having a new life in Christ.

Born Again Christian

Born Again Christian

The Pastor has a big responsibility down at the church on Hill Street.

But she has a foot problem: the shoes that she is wearing are way too big for her feet.

Leaders in the church with a special calling on their life, and that's why they have to live their life right. But she has trouble in the morning and trouble in the evening.

She keeps dreaming of an Angel, every week before she gets ready to preach, telling her what God said in her bed.

"God will shut your mouth, so that you cannot speak." The Angel said.

"Who called you to Preach? You called yourself from the start: you know that God is not dwelling in your heart. With all of your chatter, you act like Jesus dying for your sins didn't even matter. Where are you going: To Hell if you don't change your life, and come out of sin. You know that you never got saved yourself. So you really cannot save anybody else. "

The Pastor has a big responsibility down at the church on Hill Street.

But she has a foot problem: the shoes that she is wearing are way too big for her feet.

She is afraid now to wake up and get out of her bed, because every time she is standing in front of the church speaking to her congregation,

she can see the Angel of the Lord sitting in the back seat.

Finally, she woke up and hurried inside of the church,

and stood in front of the congregation. And as usual,

The Angel of the Lord did something new; he stands up from his seat and shout's that you have a confession to make.

Now by this time the Pastor is trembling with fear and she said to herself, I hope the congregation did not hear. But suddenly her worst fear grabbed hold of her in her mind, she began thinking, maybe the congregation can really hear the Angel of the Lord this time.

The pastor has a big responsibility down at the church on Hill Street.

But she has a foot problem: the shoes that she is wearing are way too big for her feet.

She fell on her knees and said oh Lord, Please help me, please. I don't want to die, I want to live. I Have so much to give. Lord, change my ways because I'm not playing, I really need to be saved.

Many of the people in the church were teary eyed and some people were silent and looking shocked. But some people started getting up from their seats with angry looks, walking outside.

When she broke down, one woman in the congregation stood up and looked around and said, what's wrong with our Pastor, why did she fall down on her knees? I'm here for you Pastor if you need some motivation. The woman that stood up doesn't understand that her Pastor needs salvation.

But the Pastor remembers her dream from Last night, and what the Angel of the Lord told her

to do. The Pastor got up off her knees and shouted to her congregation what the Angel said.

He said to me, where are you going: To Hell if you don't change your life, and come out of sin.

You know that you never got saved yourself. So you really cannot save anybody else.

The pastor has a big responsibility down at the church on Hill Street.

But she has a foot problem: the shoes that she is wearing are way too big for her feet.

About the Author

Tonya Latrice Wilson attended Columbia College in Chicago IL, and received her Bachelor's of Arts in Fiction Writing.

Born Again Christian, the first series, is her second book of published poetry.

in   Chicago   and

majored   Born   Again

Christian, the first series,

is her second book of

published poetry.

www.ingramcontent.com/pod-product-compliance
Lightning Source LLC
Chambersburg PA
CBHW021922040426
42448CB00007B/865